# just

A LITTLE BOOK **OF LIQUID SUNSHINE**

**MARGARITAS & SANGRIAS.**

Cheryl Charming

*Photographs by Susan Bourgoin*

Lyons Press
Guilford, Connecticut

*An imprint of Globe Pequot Press*

To buy books in quantity for corporate use
or incentives, call **(800) 962-0973**
or e-mail **premiums@GlobePequot.com**.

The following manufacturers/names appearing in *Just Margaritas and Sangrias* are trademarks: Alizé® Red Passion, Clase Azul Ultra Tequila, Chambord®, Cointreau®, Curaçao, DiSaronno® Amaretto, Fresca®, Grand Marnier®, Grand Marnier® Cuvée Speciale Cent Cinquantenaire, Grand Marnier® Cent du Centenaire, Jose Cuervo®, Karo, Lambrusco®, Midori, Monin, POM Wonderful LLC, Southern Comfort®, Splenda®, Tequila Rose, Tuaca

Photos on the following pages are courtesy of Shutterstock.com: page iv © iodrakon; page 50 © Pinkcandy.

Prop Credits:
Bar tools and products provided by www.barproducts.com.
Cocktail sticks, picks, straws, and drink decoration novelties provided by Spirit Foodservice, Inc. (www.spirit foodservice.com).

Text design by Georgiana Goodwin

Library of Congress Cataloging-in-Publication Data
Charming, Cheryl.
  Just margaritas and sangrias : a little book of liquid sunshine / Cheryl Charming ; photographs by Susan Bourgoin.
    p. cm.
  Includes index.
  ISBN 978-1-59921-898-4
  1. Margaritas. 2. Cocktails. I. Title.
  TX951.C4676 2009
  641.8'74—dc22

                                                                              2009043603

Printed in China

10 9 8 7 6 5 4 3 2 1

With many things in life, simpler is better.

And this holds true for the margarita. As a matter of fact, the margarita is the most popular cocktail in the world. A true margarita is simply tequila, orange liqueur, and fresh lime juice shaken and then strained into a cocktail glass. That's it. Using these three ingredients at a ratio of 3:2:1 is ideal.

The orange liqueur should be all the sweetness a true margarita needs, but a laid-back singer named Jimmy Buffett had a hit song in the 1970s entitled "Margaritaville" that caused sweet fake lime margarita premixes to be marketed to meet consumer demand. In the mixer aisle today, you have choices consisting of sour mix, sweet-and-sour mix, limeade, and margarita mix, but the very best mix is home-made. (Learn to make your own on page 97.)

As for orange liqueur, you can use triple sec or Curaçao. Triple sec is an orange liqueur that has been distilled three times (triple), and the word *sec* is French for "dry." A high-end French triple sec is Cointreau (pronounced QWAN-twoh). Grand Marnier is an orange liqueur but with a cognac base. Curaçao (pronounced cure-uh-SOW, rhymes with now) is made on the Caribbean island of the same name and comes in three colors: orange, blue, and green.

Everything in life has levels from low to high, and the margarita is no exception. By bumping up the quality of tequila and orange liqueur, you'll create a taste with depth and character. The first thing to look for on the tequila label is "100 percent blue agave." The label may read just "100 percent agave." Next, you want it to be either a *blanco* or a *reposado*. The blanco also uses the marketing terms "silver" or "white." An *añejo* will be more expensive because it is aged longer and filtered more times, but it will have too smooth a taste, causing it to blend instead of balance the acid of the lime. The blanco or reposado

Basically, *gold tequila* is a marketing term that means a category of tequila called *joven*. Jovens are just blanco tequilas that have had fake coloring added to make them look gold. Consumers then think that they are purchasing aged tequila because aging in barrels is what turns spirits amber gold. The most popular joven is Jose Cuervo.

will provide the bite to balance the flavors. Save the añejo for sipping (see page 115).

Adding an extra flavor to the simple and basic recipe of a margarita adds fun and flair. These fruity flavors are found in almost every bar across America. Injecting the extra fruity flavor can be done in many ways. The flavor can come from juices, fruits, purees, nectars, liqueurs, and even flavored tequilas. Flavors that work well in a margarita are strawberry, raspberry, melon, peach, mango, coconut, orange, and pineapple.

If you are using a flavored liqueur as your flavoring agent, then simply replace the orange liqueur with the flavored liqueur. When using all other flavorings, you keep the orange liqueur in the recipe. If you use a flavored liqueur, flavored tequila, or juice in a fruity margarita, then you have the option to make them up, on the rocks, or frozen. When using puree and nectar flavors, you could make them up or on the rocks, but they work best when made frozen because they are thicker.

Normally you don't salt the rim on a fruity margarita; however, some people like the salt on a sweeter margarita. Others will rim the glass in sugar, and still others will make a 1:1 mixture of salt and sugar to rim with. The bottom line is preference (see page 109).

You can also combine fruity flavors that complement each other for extra flavor and fun. Certain flavors simply blend together well. A great example is chocolate and peanut butter, but don't worry: You won't be making a chocolate–peanut butter margarita! Combining complementary flavors is the next progressive step to creating unique fruity margaritas. Try strawberry-kiwi, peach-papaya, blueberry-mint, mandarin-coconut, watermelon-pepper, or even raspberry-lemon for starters.

You can also find an assortment of infused and flavored tequilas with these flavors: coconut, pomegranate, citrus, coffee, chili, mango, almond, and berry. Of course, you can always infuse your own tequila by learning how on page 99.

As for unique rims for margaritas, you can always make colored salt and flavored salt. To color the salt, simply put half a cup of coarse salt and one drop of food coloring into a plastic bag, then shake. Flavors can be added the same way by using extracts, syrups, juice, and citrus zest. You can also purchase colored salts. Other dry stocks can be mixed with the salt, too, such as chili powder, cinnamon, ground coffee, ground peppercorns, and edible gold and silver flake (see page 109).

Global themed margaritas can be great to serve at theme parties or just to have fun creating new ones! Basically, you are just adding an ingredient that represents a country, city, state, province, region, town, county, village, district, borough, hamlet, kingdom . . . well, you get the point ●

# Original Margarita

**INGREDIENTS**

Ice
2 ounces 100 percent agave blanco tequila
1$\frac{1}{2}$ ounces triple sec
1 ounce fresh lime juice

1. Chill a 4-6-ounce cocktail glass with ice.

2. Shake ingredients with ice.

3. Strain into the chilled cocktail glass.

4. You can replace the triple sec with Cointreau.

Cocktail researchers say that a salted rim was never part of the Original Margarita recipe and probably was used later to mask the taste of cheap tequila being added to the drink. Rimming half the glass can please all preferences. At the grocery store, look for choices labeled "coarse sea salt," "margarita salt," or "kosher salt," not table salt.

# Classic Margarita

**INGREDIENTS**

Salt to rim glass (optional)
Ice
2 ounces 100 percent agave tequila of choice
1 ounce triple sec
1 ounce fresh lime juice
1 ounce simple syrup*
Lime garnish

1.  Chill a 7-ounce cocktail glass with ice.

2.  Shake ingredients with ice.

3.  Strain into the chilled cocktail glass. Add garnish.

4.  You can replace the triple sec with Cointreau.

MARGARITAS

*See page 105.

# Margarita on the Rocks

**INGREDIENTS**

Salt to rim glass (optional)
Ice
2 ounces 100 percent tequila of choice
1 ounce triple sec
1 ounce fresh lime juice
1 ounce simple syrup
Lime garnish

1. Rim a margarita glass with salt if desired.

2. Fill the margarita glass with ice.

3. Shake ingredients with ice.

4. Strain into the glass. Add garnish.

5. Shake the ingredients with ice, then strain into salted margarita glass of ice.

# Frozen Margarita

**INGREDIENTS**

Salt to rim glass (optional)
Ice
2 ounces tequila of choice
1 ounce triple sec
1 ounce fresh lime juice
1 ounce simple syrup
Lime garnish

1. Rim a margarita glass with salt if desired.

2. Blend ingredients with a half cup of ice. Add additional ice if needed.

3. Pour into margarita glass. Add garnish.

4. You can replace the triple sec with Cointreau.

# Gold Margarita

**INGREDIENTS**

Salt to rim glass (optional)
Ice
2 ounces reposado tequila of choice
1 ounce Cointreau
1 ounce fresh lime juice
1 ounce simple syrup
Lime garnish

1. **Up:** Shake ingredients with ice. Strain into a chilled cocktail glass.

2. **Rocks:** Shake ingredients with ice. Strain into a margarita glass filled with ice.

3. **Frozen:** Blend juice and syrup with a half cup of ice. Pour into a margarita glass. Top with the alcohol. Stir.

# Top-Shelf Margarita

**INGREDIENTS**

Salt to rim glass (optional)
Ice
2 ounces reposado tequila of choice
1/2 ounce Cointreau
1/2 ounce Grand Marnier
1 ounce fresh lime juice
1 ounce simple syrup
Lime garnish

1. **Up:** Shake ingredients with ice. Strain into a chilled cocktail glass.

2. **Rocks:** Shake ingredients with ice. Strain into a margarita glass filled with ice.

3. **Frozen:** Blend juice and syrup with a half cup of ice. Pour into a margarita glass. Top with the alcohol. Stir.

> If you love your margarita frozen/blended, then the best way to make it is to blend only the nonalcoholic portion, pour it into the glass, leaving room at the top, then pour the alcohol portion on top. Blending requires ice, which is just frozen water, so the flavor of the quality tequila gets watered down when you blend it.

# Millionaire Margarita

**INGREDIENTS**

Edible gold flake salt to rim glass
Ice
2 ounces Clase Azul Ultra Tequila
1 ounce Grand Marnier Cuvée Speciale Cent
  Cinquantenaire
1 ounce fresh organic lime juice
1 ounce simple syrup

1.  **Up:** Shake ingredients with ice. Strain into a
    chilled cocktail glass.

2.  **Rocks:** Shake ingredients with ice. Strain into
    a margarita glass filled with ice.

3.  **Frozen:** Blend juice and syrup with a half cup
    of ice. Pour into a margarita glass. Top with
    the alcohol. Stir.

---

### Royal Tequila

Grand Marnier Cuvée Speciale Cent Cinquantenaire is made with 50-year-old cognac
sealed by hand in a handpainted bottle. It
sells for about $225. Or buy the Cuvée du
Centenaire, made with 25-year-old cognac,
for about $175. The Clase Azul Ultra Tequila
sells for about $1,200 a bottle.

# Strawberry Margarita

**INGREDIENTS**

Ice
2 ounces 100 percent blanco tequila of choice
1 ounce triple sec
1 ounce fresh lime juice
1 ounce simple syrup
2 ounces strawberry mix or puree
Lime and strawberry garnish

1. Blend ingredients with a half cup of ice. Add additional ice if needed.

2. Pour into a margarita glass. Add garnish.

3. You can replace the triple sec with Cointreau.

### Strawberry Mix

Strawberry liqueurs are rarely used in a strawberry margarita. Most bars don't stock them, and most liquor stores don't carry them. Learn to make homemade strawberry puree on page 101. Or use lots of fresh, ripe strawberries and a little more simple syrup.

# Melon Margarita

**INGREDIENTS**

Ice
2 ounces 100 percent blanco tequila of choice
1 ounce melon liqueur
$1/10$ ounce fresh lime juice
1 ounce simple syrup
Lime garnish

1. Blend ingredients with a half cup of ice. Add additional ice if needed.

2. Pour into a margarita glass. Add garnish.

3. You can replace the blanco tequila with reposado tequila.

For every liqueur on the market, there are low-end and high-end choices. Sometimes you can get by with the lower end if you are on a budget. However, when it comes to melon liqueur, it's best to go with Midori. Generic brands can't compare. It's been around since 1978 and came from Japan. The word *midori* is Japanese for "green."

# Peach Margarita

**INGREDIENTS**

Ice
2 ounces 100 percent blanco tequila
1 ounce triple sec
$\frac{1}{10}$ ounce fresh lime juice
1 ounce simple syrup
2 ounces peach puree
$\frac{1}{2}$ ounce grenadine
Peach and lime garnish

1. Blend ingredients (except the grenadine) with a half cup of ice.

2. Pour grenadine into the bottom of the glass.

3. Pour the blended mixture into the glass. Add garnish.

4. You can replace the triple sec with Cointreau.

# Blue Coconut Margarita

**INGREDIENTS**

Ice
2 ounces coconut tequila
1 ounce blue Curaçao
$\frac{1}{10}$ ounce fresh lime juice
1 ounce simple syrup
Shredded coconut rim for glass

1. Rim a margarita glass with shredded coconut.

2. Blend ingredients with a half cup of ice. Add additional ice if needed.

3. Pour into a margarita glass.

Rimming with coconut flakes requires a little more sticking power than does just rubbing a lemon or lime around the rim and then dipping. And even though simple syrup is very sticky, it's just not quite sticky enough. You'll have to use Karo light syrup. Pour an ounce of Karo syrup onto a saucer, squeeze one lime wedge, and mix together.

# Pomegranate Mango Margarita

**INGREDIENTS**

Ice
2 ounces reposado tequila
1 ounce triple sec
1 ounce fresh lime juice
1 ounce simple syrup
1 ounce mango puree
$1/2$ ounce pomegranate juice

1. Blend ingredients with a cup of ice. Add additional ice if needed.

2. Pour into a margarita glass.

3. You can replace the triple sec with Cointreau.

# Sunrise Margarita

**INGREDIENTS**

Ice
2 ounces reposado tequila
1 ounce triple sec
1 ounce fresh lime juice
1 ounce orange juice
1 ounce simple syrup
1/2 ounce grenadine

1. Fill a margarita glass with ice.

2. Shake ingredients (except the grenadine) with ice.

3. Strain into the glass. Add grenadine.

4. You can replace the triple sec with Cointreau.

### Mexican Wedding

The Sunrise Margarita is a great marriage of two of the most popular tequila drinks in the world: tequila sunrise and a margarita. Both came out of Mexico, and each has a list of people claiming to be its inventor. They were also huge hits in the 1970s after the Eagles and Jimmy Buffett mentioned them in hit songs.

# Hawaiian Margarita

**INGREDIENTS**

Ice
2 ounces 100 percent agave blanco tequila
1 ounce triple sec
1 ounce fresh lime juice
1 ounce pineapple juice
1 ounce papaya puree
1/2 ounce simple syrup
Pineapple garnish

1. **Up:** Shake ingredients with ice. Strain into a chilled cocktail glass.

2. **Rocks:** Shake ingredients with ice. Strain into a margarita glass filled with ice.

3. **Frozen:** Blend ingredients with a half cup of ice. Pour into a margarita glass.

What makes the Hawaiian Margarita Hawaiian is the pineapple and papaya because both are grown in Hawaii. You can replace the papaya with other Hawaiian fruits such as banana, coconut, or mango. This margarita can be served at a tiki-, tropical-, or luau-themed party. Feel free to garnish the drink with plenty of edible flowers and paper parasols.

# Italian Margarita

**INGREDIENTS**

Ice
2 ounces 100 percent agave tequila of choice
1 ounce DiSaronno Originale Amaretto
1 ounce fresh lime juice
$1/2$ simple syrup
Pineapple garnish

1. **Up:** Shake ingredients with ice. Strain into a chilled cocktail glass.

2. **Rocks:** Shake ingredients with ice. Strain into a margarita glass filled with ice.

3. **Frozen:** Blend all but Amaretto with a half cup of ice. Pour into a margarita glass. Top with Amaretto. Stir.

# Southern Margarita

**INGREDIENTS**

Ice
2 ounces reposado tequila
1 ounce Southern Comfort (SoCo)
1 ounce fresh lime juice
1 ounce simple syrup
Lime garnish

1. **Up:** Shake ingredients with ice. Strain into a chilled cocktail glass.

2. **Rocks:** Shake ingredients with ice. Strain into a margarita glass filled with ice.

3. **Frozen:** Blend all but SoCo with a half cup of ice. Pour into a margarita glass. Top with the SoCo. Stir.

Many people will find it interesting to know that there is not one drop of whiskey inside Southern Comfort. It's a high-proof liqueur made from peach, apricot, and secret spices. It was invented by a New Orleans bartender, Martin Wilkes Heron, in 1874. It won a gold medal at the 1904 St. Louis World's Fair.

# French Margarita

**INGREDIENTS**

Ice
2 ounces reposado tequila
1 ounce Chambord
1 ounce fresh lime juice
1 ounce simple syrup
Lime garnish

1. **Up:** Shake ingredients with ice. Strain into a chilled cocktail glass.

2. **Rocks:** Shake ingredients with ice. Strain into a margarita glass filled with ice.

3. **Frozen:** Blend ingredients with a half cup of ice. Pour into a margarita glass. Add more Chambord if desired.

# Bed of Roses Margarita

**INGREDIENTS**

Ice
1 ounce reposado tequila
2 ounces Tequila Rose liqueur
1 ounce fresh lime juice
$1/2$ ounce simple syrup
Rose petals and lime garnish

1. Blend ingredients with a half cup of ice.

2. Pour into a margarita glass. Add garnish.

3. You can also rim the glass with shredded rose petals if desired.

### Tequila Rose

Tequila Rose is a tequila-based strawberry cream liqueur. It tastes a little like melted strawberry ice cream, so this margarita will taste like a creamy strawberry margarita. The drink will turn out pink in color. The color of rose petals used as a fun garnish is up to you or what you have available. Make sure to wash them.

# Guacamole Margarita

**INGREDIENTS**

Salt to rim glass
Ice
2 ounces reposado tequila
1 ounce Cointreau
$\frac{1}{2}$ ounce fresh lime juice
$\frac{1}{2}$ ounce fresh lemon juice
1 ounce simple syrup
$\frac{1}{2}$ ripe avocado (plus $\frac{1}{2}$ for garnish)
Avocado slice, and cilantro sprig garnish

1. Rim a margarita glass with salt.

2. Blend ingredients with a half cup of ice.

3. Pour into a margarita glass. Add garnish.
   Garnish can include a lime slice as well.

# Jalapeño Marmalade Margarita

**INGREDIENTS**

Ice
2 ounces reposado tequila
1 ounce Grand Marnier or Cointreau
1 ounce fresh lime juice
1 ounce orange marmalade
$\frac{1}{2}$ jalapeño or whole if you like the heat
Whole jalapeño garnish

1. Blend ingredients with a cup of ice. Add additional ice if needed.

2. Pour into a margarita glass. Add garnish.

3. You can add more fresh lime juice to taste.

It's best to use gloves when handling jalapeños. If you don't have gloves, then pay special attention at all times because their oil can be hot. The most common mistake is forgetting you've touched an exposed jalapeño, then rubbing an eye or other body part. Wash your hands after your exposure with them, especially around children.

# Skinny Margarita

**INGREDIENTS**

Salt to rim glass (optional)
Ice
1½ ounces tequila
Capful of orange extract
1 ounce lime juice
1 ounce sugar-free simple syrup

1. **Up:** Shake ingredients with ice. Strain into a chilled cocktail glass.

2. **Rocks:** Shake ingredients with ice. Strain into a margarita glass filled with ice.

3. **Frozen:** Blend ingredients with a half cup of ice. Pour into a margarita glass.

# Natural SeñoRita

**INGREDIENTS**

Ice
1½ ounces organic tequila
1 ounce organic orange juice
1 ounce organic lime juice
1 ounce organic raw simple syrup
Optional organic sea salt rim and lime garnish

1. **Up:** Shake ingredients with ice. Strain into a chilled cocktail glass.

2. **Rocks:** Shake ingredients with ice. Strain into a margarita glass filled with ice.

3. **Frozen:** Blend ingredients with a half cup of ice. Pour into a margarita glass.

The Natural SeñoRita is basically an organic margarita with organic orange juice used to substitute the orange liqueur. You can also use other organic juices in its place. Pomegranate would be nice. Other substitutions include Monin organic raspberry syrup, organic fruits, purees, or organic jams and jellies. While you're at it, you can infuse the tequila with many flavors, too!

Sangria in its basic form is just wine, fruit, juices, and spirit mixed together and topped with something bubbly.

Although no one knows when the first sangria was made, it's believed to be a longtime social drink that came from Spain. A Spanish housewife probably needed to make a batch for a festive evening with friends, then looked at her pantry inventory and voilà! (excuse the French), sangria was born.

The ideal way to prepare sangria is to allow most of the fruits to sit overnight in the fridge to soak up the alcohol and flavor, but you can cheat and make it a few hours ahead as well. Fruits used mostly as decoration such as star fruit, for example, can be added right before serving.

The traditional red wine used in Spain for sangrias is rioja. The desired overall taste of sangria is slightly sweet. Different wines have different sweetness levels, but don't fret. If the sangria is too sour, then add more sweetener, and if it's too sweet, then add a sour with more citrus juice. You'll notice decorated sangria bottles on the bottom shelf in the wine aisle. You don't want to buy these premixes. These are for people who know nothing about sangria. Besides, they contain too much sugar and preservatives. Making your own is always better! However, the Lambrusco wine sitting next to these sangria premixes is worth using in sangria. Remember that the wine you use can also be organic or alcohol free. Alcohol-free choices are great for children, pregnant women, designated drivers, and other people who can't have or don't want alcohol. You could always make one pitcher of nonalcoholic sangria and label it. Don't forget to leave out the spirit/liqueur portion as well.

Practically any liquor, liqueur, juice, spice, fruit, or carbonation is possible. As for spirits, you can use brandy, vodka, rum, gin, tequila, and whiskey in flavors available. Liqueur choices abound, and juices can also be replaced with nectars and purees. More flavor combinations to try include kiwi-strawberry, mango-vanilla, spiced pear, pineapple-ginger, raspberry-lychee, tangerine-clove, apple-Amaretto, and chili-lime.

To add a zing for your guests, you can also get creative by freezing fun edibles in ice cubes. You could make ice cubes with cherries, berries, pomegranate seeds or chopped apples, and lemons. Simply drop your edible choice into the cavities of the ice trays, then fill with water and freeze. Continue the process over a number of days until you collect a nice big bowl of them in the freezer. That is, unless you have a large freezer and many trays to freeze at one time.

Without a doubt, sangria is a libation meant to be shared with friends and family. When having guests over, it's best to designate a drink area that can be accessed from all four sides to encourage mingling and conversation. Always have this area decorated to match your theme and stocked with everything a guest may need. Ice scoops and a trash can may sound minor, but they are tools that will be used.

If you like traditional red sangria, then you will love the white version! Some people prefer it because it has a translucency that allows the beautiful fruit to shine through. White sangria is also known as "Sangria Blanco," and the best wine to use for a Sangria Blanco is a dry wine like Sauvignon Blanc. This way

SANGRIAS

the dryness of the wine will balance with the sweetness added to it. If you use a sweeter white wine like a Riesling or Chardonnay, then balance the sweetness by adding more lemon or lime juice and omitting the sugar.

These days you'll find stores on the Internet that sell anything you want in the color pink. So why not have a pink sangria? Pink sangrias are perfect for a girls' night in, baby shower, bridal shower, bachelorette party, or for the person who loves pink or an event that is represented by the color pink. Wine choices include White Zinfandel, Rosé, and pink Champagne.

### Sangria Tips

- Less expensive wine works fine.
- Go seasonal with the fruit.
- Serve over ice in garnished wine glasses.
- Explore the many choices of carbonation available.
- Try serving with bamboo skewers so that the fruit can be speared and eaten by your guests.

Have fun and come up with your own theme sangrias! Ideas to spark your imagination include the Color Purple Sangria with violet syrup with plums and grapes, Billy Joel Sangria with a bottle of red and a bottle of white, or Kitchen Sink Sangria with whatever you have in your kitchen ●

# Spanish Sangria

**INGREDIENTS**

1 750-milliliter bottle rioja
$\frac{1}{2}$ cup Spanish brandy
1 cup orange juice
$\frac{1}{2}$ cup lemon juice
$\frac{1}{4}$ cup sugar or simple syrup
Orange slices
2 oranges and 2 lemons, sliced, for garnish
Ice
24 ounces soda water

YIELDS 8 SERVINGS

1. Pour the first five ingredients into a pitcher or large container. Stir.

2. Add orange slices and let sit in the fridge for 3–12 hours.

3. When ready, pour about 6 ounces of sangria into fruit-garnished wine glasses half filled with ice.

4. Top each glass with 3 ounces soda water.

# Italian Sangria

**INGREDIENTS**

1 750-milliliter bottle Italian red wine
$\frac{1}{2}$ cup grappa
1 cup orange juice
$\frac{1}{2}$ cup lemon juice
$\frac{1}{4}$ cup sugar or simple syrup
Orange and peach slices
2 oranges and 2 lemons, sliced, for garnish
24 ounces soda water
Ice

YIELDS 8 SERVINGS

1. Pour first five ingredients into a pitcher. Stir.

2. Add orange, peach slices; let sit in fridge 3–12 hours.

3. When ready, pour 6 ounces sangria into fruit-garnished wine glasses half filled with ice.

4. Top each glass with 3 ounces soda water.

# French Sangria

**INGREDIENTS**

1 750-milliliter bottle French red wine
1/2 cup Grand Marnier
1 cup orange juice
1/2 cup lemon juice
1/4 cup sugar or simple syrup
Orange slices
2 oranges and 2 lemons, sliced, and 1/2 pint
   raspberries for garnish
24 ounces soda water
Ice

YIELDS 8 SERVINGS

1. Pour first five ingredients into pitcher. Stir. Add slices; let sit in fridge 3–12 hours.

2. When ready, pour 6 ounces sangria into fruit-garnished wine glasses half filled with ice.

3. Top each glass with 3 ounces soda water.

> One of the keys to sangria is the way you present the fruit. So think about the various ways you can cut fruit for the prettiest presentation. You can make balls, triangles, squares, or circles from various fruits.

# Chocolate Cherry Sangria

**INGREDIENTS**

1 750-milliliter bottle red wine
1/2 cup cherry brandy
1/2 cup white crème de cacao
1/2 cup lemon juice
1 cup maraschino or fresh cherries
Ice
24 ounces black cherry soda

YIELDS 8 SERVINGS

1. Pour the first four ingredients into a pitcher. Stir.

2. Add cherries and juice.

3. When ready, pour about 6 ounces of sangria into fruit-garnished wine glasses half filled with ice.

4. Top each glass with 3 ounces black cherry soda.

# Blackberry Apple Maple Sangria

**INGREDIENTS**

1 750-milliliter bottle red wine
1/2 cup blackberry brandy
1/2 cup apple juice or cider
1/2 cup lemon juice
1/4 cup maple syrup
1 pint blackberries and 2 red apples, diced
2 lemons, sliced
Ice
24 ounces lemon-lime soda

YIELDS 8 SERVINGS

1. Pour the first five ingredients into a pitcher. Stir.

2. Add blackberries and apples.

3. When ready, pour 6 ounces sangria into lemon-garnished wine glasses half filled with ice.

4. Top each glass with 3 ounces lemon-lime soda.

# Raspberry Pom Peach Sangria

**INGREDIENTS**

1 750-milliliter bottle red wine
$1/2$ cup peach schnapps
$1/2$ cup pomegranate juice
$1/2$ cup lemon juice
2 peaches, sliced
2 lemons, sliced
$1/2$ pint raspberries
Ice
24 ounces raspberry-flavored soda

YIELDS 8 SERVINGS

1. Pour the first four ingredients into a pitcher. Stir.

2. Add peaches.

3. When ready, pour 6 ounces sangria into lemon- and raspberry-garnished wine glasses half filled with ice.

4. Top each glass with 3 ounces raspberry-flavored soda.

> For all sangrias, add fruit after initial ingredients and then let sit in the fridge 3–12 hours before serving.

# Red Chai Sangria

**INGREDIENTS**

1 750-milliliter bottle red wine
1/2 cup Tuaca
1/2 cup apple juice or cider
1/2 cup lemon juice
2 red apples, diced
Teaspoon of ground cinnamon
Medium bag of red hots (cinnamon candy)
Ice
24 ounces cream soda

YIELDS 8 SERVINGS

1. Pour the first four ingredients into a pitcher. Stir.

2. Add apples.

3. When ready, pour 6 ounces sangria into cinnamon and red hot–garnished wine glasses half filled with ice.

4. Top each glass with 3 ounces cream soda.

# Fiesta Sangria

**INGREDIENTS**

1 750-milliliter bottle red wine
½ cup tequila
½ cup pineapple juice
½ cup orange juice
½ cup lime juice
¼ cup agave syrup
An assortment of colorful fruits
Ice
24 ounces lemon-lime soda

YIELDS 8 SERVINGS

1. Pour first six ingredients into a pitcher. Stir.

2. Add an assortment of fruit.

3. When ready, pour 6 ounces sangria into fruit-garnished wine glasses half filled with ice.

4. Top each glass with 3 ounces lemon-lime soda.

> The spirit used for Fiesta Sangria is tequila. Agave syrup is also called "agave nectar" and is made from the agave plant (which is the plant that tequila is made from).

# Passionate Summer Holiday Sangria

**INGREDIENTS**

1 750-milliliter bottle red wine
1/2 cup Alizé Red Passion liqueur
1/2 cup pineapple juice
1/2 cup lemon juice
1/4 cup honey syrup
1 pint strawberries and 1 cup seedless grapes
Ice
24 ounces pink Champagne

YIELDS 8 SERVINGS

1. Pour first five ingredients into a pitcher. Stir.

2. Add some of the fruit.

3. When ready, pour 6 ounces sangria into fruit-garnished wine glasses half filled with ice.

4. Top each glass with 3 ounces pink Champagne.

# Midnight at the Oasis Sangria

**INGREDIENTS**

1 750-milliliter bottle red wine
$1/2$ cup pineapple vodka
$1/2$ cup tangerine juice
$1/2$ cup lemon juice
$1/4$ cup raw sugar or raw sugar simple syrup
2 oranges, sliced
Pineapple, sliced
1 cup pineapple fronds
1 star fruit
Ice
24 ounces lemon-lime soda

YIELDS 8 SERVINGS

1. Pour first five ingredients into a pitcher. Stir.

2. Add oranges and pineapple.

3. When ready, pour 6 ounces sangria into fruit-garnished wine glasses half filled with ice.

4. Top each glass with 3 ounces lemon-lime soda.

The Midnight at the Oasis Sangria would be wonderful to serve at an Arabian or desert theme party.

# Classic White Sangria

**INGREDIENTS**

1 cup apple juice
1/2 cup lemon juice
1 cup water
1/4 cup sugar or simple syrup
2 cinnamon sticks
1 750-milliliter bottle cava white wine
2 oranges, sliced
2 red apples, diced
2 lemons, sliced
Ice
24 ounces soda water

YIELDS 8 SERVINGS

1. Slowly heat juices, water, sugar, and cinnamon sticks for 15 minutes. Add wine and half the fruit; stir. Chill 3–12 hours.

2. When ready, pour 6 ounces sangria into (remaining) fruit-garnished wine glasses half filled with ice.

3. Top each glass with 3 ounces soda water.

# White Pear-adise Sangria

**INGREDIENTS**

1 750-milliliter bottle dry white wine
$1/2$ cup pear brandy
$1/2$ cup white grape juice
$1/2$ cup lemon juice
$1/4$ cup honey
2 pears, diced
2 lemons, sliced
1 pint strawberries for garnish
Ice
24 ounces lemon-lime soda

YIELDS 8 SERVINGS

1. Pour first five ingredients into a pitcher. Stir.

2. Add pears.

3. When ready, pour 6 ounces sangria into lemon- and strawberry-garnished wine glasses half filled with ice.

4. Top with 3 ounces lemon-lime soda.

The pear brandy in the White Pear-adise Sangria can be substituted with pear schnapps or pear vodka.

# White Granny Smith Mint Sangria

**INGREDIENTS**

1 750-milliliter bottle dry white wine
1/2 cup sour apple vodka
1 cup white cranberry juice
1/2 cup lemon juice
1/4 cup sugar or simple syrup
1 cup peppermint sprigs
2 Granny Smith apples, diced
2 lemons, sliced
Ice
24 ounces soda water

YIELDS 8 SERVINGS

1. Pour first five ingredients into a pitcher. Stir.

2. Add mint and apples to sangria.

3. When ready, pour 6 ounces sangria into lemon-garnished wine glasses half filled with ice. Top each glass with 3 ounces soda water.

> The White Granny Smith Mint Sangria can use sour apple schnapps in place of the sugar for a more intense green apple taste. The color, of course, will change as well.

# Tropical Luau Sangria

**INGREDIENTS**

1 750-milliliter bottle dry white wine
$1/2$ cup coconut rum
$1/2$ cup white grape juice
$1/2$ cup pineapple juice
$1/2$ cup lemon juice
$1/4$ cup falernum syrup
Assorted tropical fruits
Flowers
Ice
24 ounces lemon-lime soda

YIELDS 8 SERVINGS

1. Pour the first six ingredients into a pitcher. Stir.

2. Add the fruit.

3. When ready, pour 6 ounces sangria into wine glasses half filled with ice and garnish with flowers.

4. Top with 3 ounces lemon-lime soda.

# Patriotic Sangria

**INGREDIENTS**

1 750-milliliter bottle dry American white wine
½ cup strawberry vodka
1 cup apple juice
½ cup lemon juice
¼ cup sugar or simple syrup
Strawberries, blueberries, and star fruit
Ice
24 ounces lemon-lime soda

YIELDS 8 SERVINGS

1. Pour first five ingredients into a pitcher. Stir.

2. Pour 6 ounces sangria into fruit-garnished wine glasses half filled with ice.

3. Top each glass with 3 ounces lemon-lime soda.

> The goal of the Patriotic Sangria is to match the colors of the country of your choice; in this case, the country is America with blueberries, strawberries, and stars. France's colors are red, white, and blue, too, so the drink can be modified with French white wine.

# Pool Party Sangria

**INGREDIENTS**

1 750-milliliter bottle dry white wine
½ cup blue Curaçao
1 cup white grape juice
½ cup lemon juice
2 lemons and 2 oranges, sliced
1 pint of blueberries
1 cup of seedless grapes
Ice
24 ounces lemon-lime soda

YIELDS 8 SERVINGS

1. Pour first four ingredients into a pitcher. Stir.

2. Add fruit.

3. When ready, pour 6 ounces sangria into garnished wine glasses half filled with ice.

4. Top with 3 ounces lemon-lime soda.

Pool Party Sangria incorporates blue Curaçao so that it looks like pool water. Make citrus rings to look like swim rings and throw in some grapes for beach balls. If you don't have blue Curaçao, substitute it with orange liqueur and blue food coloring.

# Down Under Sangria

**INGREDIENTS**

1 750-milliliter bottle dry Australian white wine
$1/2$ cup mango vodka
1 cup white grape juice
$1/2$ cup lemon juice
$1/4$ cup sugar or simple syrup
2 kiwi, 2 papayas, and 2 mangos, peeled and
   sliced
Ice
24 ounces soda water

YIELDS 8 SERVINGS

1. Pour first five ingredients into a pitcher. Stir.

2. Add fruit.

3. When ready, pour 6 ounces sangria into
   garnished wine glasses half filled with ice.

4. Top each glass with 3 ounces soda water.

> Before you make Down Under Sangria, check
> your local grocer for kiwi. Although many
> fruits like mango, papaya, and banana grow in
> Australia, the kiwi is its mascot fruit and sim-
> ply cannot be left out of this theme sangria.

# Pretty in Pink Sangria

**INGREDIENTS**

1 750-milliliter bottle White Zinfandel wine
$1/2$ cup limoncello
$1/2$ cup white cranberry juice
$1/2$ cup pink grapefruit juice
$1/2$ cup lemon juice
2 pink grapefruits, sliced
$1/2$ cup lemon spirals
1 pint raspberries or strawberries
Ice
24 ounces Fresca grapefruit soda

YIELDS 8 SERVINGS

1. Pour first five ingredients into a pitcher. Stir.

2. Add pink grapefruit.

3. Pour 6 ounces sangria into lemon and berry-garnished wine glasses half filled with ice; top each with 3 ounces Fresca soda.

> The Pretty in Pink Sangria is very versatile and can handle fun flavor changes with ease. You can experiment using cherry vodka with cherries, raspberry vodka or rum with raspberries, grape vodka with grapes, orange vodka with oranges, pear vodka with pears, and so forth.

# Rose Parade Sangria

**INGREDIENTS**

1/2 cup cherry vodka
3/4 cup white grape juice
1/2 cup lemon juice
1/4 cup rose simple syrup
1 cup white seedless grapes, 1 cup cherries, and
   2 lemons, sliced
Ice
Rose petals
2 750-milliliter bottles rosé brut Champagne

YIELDS 8 SERVINGS

1. Pour all ingredients except pink Champagne
   into a small pitcher. Stir gently.

2. When ready, pour 2 ounces of the mixture
   into rose petal–garnished wine glasses half
   filled with ice.

3. Slowly pour about 4 ounces pink Champagne
   on top.

The Rose Parade Sangria is a little different because it combines the wine and carbonation by using Champagne (or sparkling
wine). Feel free to combine it with any flavored spirit or liqueur of your choice.

# Pink Heart Sangria

**INGREDIENTS**

1 750-milliliter bottle rosé wine
$\frac{1}{2}$ cup watermelon schnapps
1 cup white grape juice
$\frac{1}{2}$ cup lemon juice
1 cup cantaloupe balls and 2 cups watermelon
  hearts
Ice
24 ounces soda water

YIELDS 8 SERVINGS

1. Pour the first four ingredients into a pitcher or large container. Stir.

2. Add the fruit, then let sit in the fridge for 3–12 hours.

3. When ready, pour about 6 ounces of sangria into fruit-garnished wine glasses half filled with ice.

4. Top with 3 ounces soda water.

> Of course, any shape can be cut from watermelon meat, but the hearts in the Pink Heart Sangria give it a feeling that you made it with love. And love is always hip.

The first thing you should know is that margarita mix has a lime base.

You wouldn't make a whiskey sour with margarita mix, and you shouldn't make a margarita with sour mix. The next thing to know is that the mix should contain only three ingredients: water, sugar, and lime juice. That's it.

When mixing the simple syrup and juice together, your goal is to reach a balance of sweet and sour. Feel free to adjust the sweetness or sour, depending on your taste preferences. Also, don't forget that you can make a sugar-free mix by using Splenda simple syrup ●

## Margarita Mix

### INGREDIENTS

2 cups fresh lime juice
2 cups simple syrup

1. Mix the juice and simple syrup together.

2. Pour into a sterile bottle. Refrigerate.

To infuse spirits, all you need are alcohol, your chosen infusion ingredients, a wide-mouthed jar, and time.

Simply pour the spirit into a sterilized wide-mouthed jar, add the washed and rinsed edible infusion of choice, and seal the top. Set the jar in a cabinet and every day turn it upside down once and back, then set it back in the cabinet. After a few days, you can open the jar and taste-test it. Some ingredients take only three to four days (vanilla, citrus rinds, garlic), while others take up to two weeks (chilis, beans, ginger) ●

# Coffee and Cacao Bean–Infused Tequila

**INGREDIENTS**

1 750-milliliter bottle premium tequila
$\frac{1}{2}$ cup roasted coffee beans
$\frac{1}{2}$ cup cacao beans (nips)

1.  Pour tequila into a sterile, wide-mouthed jar or jars.

2.  Add coffee beans. Seal jar.

3.  Set in a dark cool place and agitate once daily for two weeks.

4.  Strain and funnel into a sterile jar or bottle.

Purees add bursting, concentrated flavor to a cocktail.

Making purees is pretty simple. Basically, you peel and chop your chosen carbohydrate, then heat it and mash it up. Heating options include baking, boiling, and steaming. The preferred method is steaming because it keeps a lot of the flavor and vitamins intact. Baking is fine, but it takes a long time and uses a lot of energy. After your puree is heated, simply use a food processor to mash it up. At this point, you can mix in more ingredients or other purees with it if desired. Then the mash gets spooned straight into small sterile jars. You can also use simple disposable plasticware. Some people prefer to push the puree through a sieve for extra straining first.

Keep the puree in the fridge for preservation. You can also freeze the puree in ice trays. When it's frozen, pop out the puree cubes and store in a freezer bag for future use. You can use them in the blender for a frozen drink or allow them to thaw ●

# Peach Puree

**INGREDIENTS**

1 pound peaches (about 4) skinned, pitted, and chopped

1 ounce simple syrup if desired

YIELDS 1 CUP

1. Steam peaches until soft.

2. Place in the food processor for 1 minute.

3. Taste, then add simple syrup if desired.

4. Spoon into sterile jars or containers. Refrigerate.

### Easy Skinning

You can skin fruit with a knife, but with some fruit it's easier to boil it first. Bring a large pot of water to a boil, then drop in the fruit. Boil for 5–10 minutes, then remove from the pot and set on a towel to cool. When it is cool, you can easily remove the skins of the fruit.

# Tropical Puree

**INGREDIENTS**

1 mango peeled, pitted, and chopped
1 cup chopped fresh pineapple
1 ripe banana
1 ounce simple syrup or falernum if desired

YIELDS 1 CUP

1. Steam mango and pineapple until soft.

2. Place in the food processor with the banana for 1 minute.

3. Taste, then add simple syrup or falernum if desired.

4. Spoon into sterile jars or containers. Refrigerate.

The tropical puree can contain any of your favorite tropical fruits, such as papaya, mandarin oranges, lychees, kiwi, and tangerines. Cornucopia puree can contain any autumn, winter, and harvest edibles such as pears, squash, ground nuts, cranberries, persimmons, oranges, and ground allspice. You could even make a spa puree with cucumber, mint, and lemons.

Simple syrup is simply sugar and water mixed together to make a liquid sugar.

Sugar in syrup form is the ideal way to add sweetness to a cocktail. Granulated sugar doesn't dissolve as well.

For the simple syrup recipe, a ratio of 1:1 works fine, but some people prefer it a little thicker and will use twice as much sugar as is called for in this recipe. You'll discover your preference after you begin to experiment. For the water, try to use the highest quality available, and for sugar you have choices of raw, organic, brown, and more.

To make infused simple syrup, you just add clean herbs, fruits, veggies, spices, and so forth to the water. Bring it to a boil, add the sugar, and stir until the sugar is dissolved. Remove from the heat, cover, and allow it to cool and steep. After about 30 minutes you can strain and funnel into a jar or bottle. Simple syrup will keep in the fridge for a month.

For a no-heat sugar-free simple syrup, use filtered room-temperature water and shake it hard with Splenda in a jar or bottle. You'll notice that the Splenda dissolves very quickly. Simply refrigerate ●

# Simple Syrup

**INGREDIENTS**

2 cups water
2 cups sugar

1. Bring the water to a boil.

2. Pour in the sugar. Stir until dissolved.

3. Remove from heat and allow cooling.

4. Funnel into a jar or bottle.

## Simple Syrup Tips

- Sterilize all jars and bottles to be used.
- Wash hands thoroughly.
- Try to buy organic and always wash and always rinse your infusion ingredients well.
- If you do not have filtered water, then boil water twice to purify.

# Tri-Citrus Infused Simple Syrup

**INGREDIENTS**

2 cups water
Zest from 1 lime, 1 lemon, and 1 orange
2 cups sugar

1. Bring the water and the citrus zest to a boil.

2. Pour in the sugar. Stir until dissolved.

3. Remove from heat and allow to cool and steep for 30 minutes.

4. Strain and funnel into a jar or bottle.

# No-Heat Simple Syrup

**INGREDIENTS**

2 cups sugar
2 cups lukewarm water

1.  Funnel the sugar and water into a bottle.

2.  Seal cap and shake hard for 10 seconds.

3.  Let sit for 1 minute, then shake hard again until sugar is dissolved. Cloudiness will clear.

Simple syrup infusions are limited only to anything that grows in the world that is not toxic. Popular infusions include vanilla, mint, ginger, citrus (use the zested rind), rose petals, lavender, and tea bags. Others to try are roasted coffee beans, peppercorns, and pumpkin. And don't forget that you can combine flavors such as vanilla ginger or cacao bean and chili.

Rimming something on the rim of a glass requires two things: something wet or sticky and your chosen edible ingredient.

Saucers and plates work well for holding your ingredients. Lemon juice mixes well with sugar-based rims, and lime juice mixes well with salted rims.

For colored and flavored rims, use plastic bags and food coloring to color salts and sugars. Visit cake and cookie decorating supply stores for a larger assortment of colorings and other edible items. Crush cookies and candy in plastic bags ●

## Sticking Power

The easiest way to wet the rim of a glass is to rub a slice of citrus around the rim. But sometimes this is not enough sticking power to hold something heavier. You may have to use simple syrup, honey, or Karo syrup. If you have time, apply it with a paintbrush.

Strive to rim the outside edge of the glass only. Salt falling into a margarita will change the taste of the drink. Flavored rims combined with the flavor of the cocktail are meant to complement each other and to enhance the taste as it reaches your lips.

A sharp knife is crucial when cutting garnishes.

A dull knife is dangerous because it can slip off the food you're cutting and cut your fingers instead. Serrated knives with little teeth that can grab hold of citrus fruit are better for beginners, and they don't need sharpening. You can keep other knives sharpened by using a long rod called a *steel* or other types of knife sharpeners.

Always make sure your hands, the knife, and what you are cutting are dry before you start cutting. When you come to a stage of cutting when the blade is getting too close to your fingers, simply curl them under while still applying firm pressure.

## CUTTING WEDGES AND WHEELS

Wheels for drink garnishes are very decorative. However, they are not practical to squeeze into a drink because of the mess doing so will make on your hands. Wedges are designed to be easily lifted off the edge of a drink and then squeezed to add flavor in one smooth motion.

Wheels can be cut from any fruit or vegetable with a circular shape. The most common is citrus.

Begin with a secure, clean surface. Cut off the end of a lemon, lime, or orange. Make a $\frac{1}{4}$-inch slice into the lengthwise part of the fruit. This slice allows the wheel to rest on the rim of a glass. Hold the fruit firmly down with one hand. Carefully slice the width of it into wheels. If you need to make several wheels or desire very thin wheels, use a kitchen slicer or mandoline.

Wedges can be cut from any fruit or vegetable with a circular shape. The most common is citrus. Begin with a secure, clean surface, then slice the fruit in half lengthwise. Make a $\frac{1}{4}$-inch slice into the meat of the fruit widthwise. This slice allows the wedge to rest on the rim of a glass. Hold the fruit firmly down with one hand. Carefully slice the length of the it at an angle. Each half should yield three or four wedges.

## CUTTING A PINEAPPLE

When cutting a pineapple, know that you will need a larger space than usual and a larger knife. You can also save the top end of the pineapple (with the fronds). It can be used as decoration in a display or bamboo-skewered fruit kebabs could stick into it. The fronds can also be torn off and used as a garnish. You'll have to trim the bottoms of them a little for the sake of visual presentation. You can also spear fronds on a pineapple slice. A fancy way to attach the fronds to a pineapple slice is to make an incision in the top of the slice, then insert a couple of fronds down into the incision point side up. For punches made with pineapple juice, just throw a handful of fronds in for fun.

## CUTTING A PINEAPPLE: STEP 1

Begin with a secure, clean surface. Slice off the ends of a pineapple. Carefully cut the pineapple in half lengthwise. Discard the ends.

## CUTTING A PINEAPPLE: STEP 2

Lay the pineapple halves flat for cutting stability. Slice both pineapple halves lengthwise. The result will be four lengthwise pineapple quarters. After some practice, you may discover that you prefer to cut the quarters in half to make eighths. This will yield more slices in the end.

## CUTTING A PINEAPPLE: STEP 3

Firmly hold down a pineapple quarter (because the outside curve of the pineapple is unstable). Make a careful $1/2$-inch lengthwise slice into a pineapple quarter. This slice allows the slice to rest on the rim of a glass. Repeat with the other three pineapple quarters. The result will be four lengthwise pineapple quarters with rim slices.

## CUTTING A PINEAPPLE: STEP 4

Turn the pineapple quarter on its flat, stable side, then hold firmly. Make many slices widthwise. Repeat with the other three pineapple quarters. The result should be 30–40 pineapple slices that will rest on the rim of a glass ●

The *numero uno* thing to know about tequila is that by law it can be produced only in the Tequila region of Mexico.

The *numero dos* thing to know is that in order for a label to say "tequila" it must be made from at least 51 percent blue agave. If it's not, then it's called a "mixto" (this is a good example of Mezcal).

## BLANCO TEQUILA

Blanco is also called "silver" or "white tequila."

Most times blanco tequila is either bottled straight out of the still or filtered, then bottled.

If stored, blanco tequila must not be kept longer than sixty days in stainless steel tanks for no aging.

### Gold Tequila

Gold tequila (also called *oro*) is a blanco tequila that has had coloring (usually cara-mel) and/or flavor added to it to make it appear that it's been aged. It's usually a mixto. The best example of this is Jose Cuervo. The term *gold* does not refer to a reposado or an añejo because they are gold in color.

One hundred percent agave blanco tequila is an excellent choice to use for margaritas.

## REPOSADO TEQUILA

Reposado is a blanco that has been aged in white oak casks for two to twelve months. It has a mellow yellow color and taste. The gold color of a reposado comes from aging in the wood casks. *Reposado* means "rested" (as in "rested in barrels").

Reposado is the highest-quality tequila that will still taste good in a margarita. It has a balance between bite and smoothness.

## AÑEJO TEQUILA

Añejo (which means "old") is a blanco tequila that has been aged for more than one year. High-quality añejos are aged up to three years.

Añejo that is aged up to eight years is called *reserva*. There is controversy over letting tequila age this long because the oak begins to overwhelm the agave flavor ●

All wines basically are one of two styles: red or white.

These styles break down into three body types: full, medium, and light. Even though there are over ten thousand types of grapes in the world, only about three hundred of these are used to make commercial wine. Out of these three hundred, twenty to thirty are used for the most popular wines. In the wine world, you will hear the word varietal often. This refers to the type of grape used. Popular red (and black) wine grapes used to make red wine include Cabernet Sauvignon, Merlot, Pinot Noir, Sangiovese, Shiraz/Syrah, Zinfandel, Gamay, Grenache, Lambrusco, Pinot Meunier, and Tempranillo.

## FULL-BODIED RED WINES

Full-bodied (sometimes called "heavy-bodied") wines are very dark in color, have a heavy feel on the tongue, and are high in tannins. The king grape of heavy-bodied wine is the Cabernet Sauvignon grape.

Other popular full-bodied red wines include Bordeaux, Malbec, and Burgundy.

Full-bodied wines are usually too strong for the beginner and are something to be graduated to.

## MEDIUM-BODIED RED WINES

Medium-bodied red wines will not be as intense as full-bodied red wines in the mouth.

The color of a medium-bodied wine will be lighter than that of a full-bodied red wine and darker than that of a light-bodied wine. A fruity taste is found with a medium-bodied wine.

Popular medium-bodied red wines include Merlot, Shiraz/Syrah, Chianti, and some Pinot Noirs.

## LIGHT-BODIED RED WINES

Light-bodied red wines are ruby red in color and often referred to as "table wines." This type of wine is good for beginners because of its light and fruity taste and feel on the tongue.

The Gamay grape is a popular grape for light-bodied red wines.

Popular light-bodied red wines include Beaujolais, Lambrusco, and some Pinot Noirs.

The first thing to know about white wine is that it can be made from white, red, purple, or even black grapes. This is because the grape skins are discarded when making white wine. With red wine, the skins are not discarded. And for pink-toned wines like White Zinfandel, Rosé, or Blush, the skins are left on just a little bit to color the wine.

Just like red wines, white wines will vary in body. They will also vary from dryness to sweetness. Popular grapes to make white wine include Chardonnay, Sauvignon Blanc, Chenin Blanc, Pinot Gris/Pinot Grigio, Pinot Blanc, Gewürztraminer, Riesling, and Viognier. All of these white wine varietals can have a dry or super sweet taste; it all depends on who grows the grapes.

## FULL-BODIED WHITE WINE

The full-bodied Chardonnay grape is the queen of the white grapes. The Chardonnay grape is the most popular white wine grape in California. It's also one of the grapes used to make Champagne.

Chardonnay is heavy, buttery, fruity, and oaky. Some winemakers don't like the oakiness of

Chardonnay, so they age the wine in stainless steel tanks.

## MEDIUM-BODIED WHITE WINE

Medium-bodied white wine is a lighter color than the heavy-bodied Chardonnay.

Popular medium-bodied white wines include Viognier, Pinot Blanc, and Gewürztraminer.

Sauvignon Blanc (also called "Fume Blanc") is probably the best example of a medium-bodied white wine.

Sauvignon Blanc has a dry, grassy, citrus, crisp taste.

## LIGHT-BODIED WHITE WINE

Light-bodied white wine is the lightest in color.

The Riesling grape originated in Germany and is Germany's leading grape varietal. Most productions have a light, sweet taste.

Popular light-bodied white wines include Chenin Blanc and Pinot Gris/Pinot Grigio.

Light-bodied wines are often drunk in the summer or at a picnic.

Organic wines have become popular, but most aren't entirely organic. Only wines with the USDA organic seal are truly made from organically grown grapes with naturally occurring sulfites. If the label says "made with organic grapes" or "made with organically grown grapes" without the seal, then sulfites have been added. It all boils down to little technical rules and regulations.

## CHAMPAGNE

Unlike most other wines, Champagnes are named after the houses that produce them.

Champagnes come in levels from sweet to dry: Doux, Demi-Sec, Sec, Extra Dry, Brut, Brut Zero, Ultra Brut, and Extra Brut.

A good temperature to serve Champagne is 44°F.

Only three grapes are used to make Champagne: Pinot Noir, Pinot Meunier, and Chardonnay.

## SPARKLING WINE

The reason why there is even a category of sparkling wine is because of the Champagne Riots in the early 1900s. The Champagne Riots resulted in a law requiring that only Champagnes made with grapes in the Champagne region could bear the word Champagne on their label.

The words *sparkling wine* can be seen on all bottles of sparkling wine made after 1927.

## PROSECCO

Prosecco is a grape used to make Italian sparkling wine. The prosecco grape is prized for its delicate flavors and aromatic taste and flavor ●